CW00570873

Inklings

300 Starts, Plots, and Challenges
to Inspire your Horror,
Science Fiction, and Fantasy Stories

Jarod K. Anderson and
Leslie J. Anderson

Copyright © 2013 by Leslie Anderson and Jarod Anderson

Cover image, 'Urban Loch Ness' copyright © 2013 Leslie Anderson

All rights reserved.

INDEX

HOW TO USE THIS BOOK

The main focus of this book is utility. We decided not to philosophize or meditate on writing, but rather simply endeavored to facilitate the process of getting started. This book is meant to be a tool, a crowbar to break into inspiration, or maybe just a blunt instrument for clubbing writer's block to death. Whatever works for you.

The book is divided into three sections: *Starts, Plots,* and *Challenges.*

Starts provide first sentences, a quick and dirty jumping off point. Here, you'll get a brief sense of tone and flow. Choose a sentence that hooks you and run with it.

Plots are rough sketches of a general narrative. They provide an overview of a conflict arch and frame a narrative skeleton upon which to build. Treat them as menu of delicious misfortunes ready to befall your unsuspecting characters.

Challenges get a little more complicated. They arm you a meta-goal for your writing, designed to force you to question your comfort zone and keep your writing fresh and challenging.

Let this book be your vault of craziness, your trusty talisman against the intimidation of the blank page, your banner of defiance against the fickle whims of the muse. In other words, this book is whatever you need it to be. Use one of the sections for a quick start, or mix two or three of them for a true writing challenge. Each suggestion in this book can produce hundreds of stories, and no two writers will approach them the same way.

What are you waiting for? Go write!

Starts

Doug didn't consider himself an "animal person," but he knew goldfish weren't typically known for their problem solving skills.

Even back when his teeth were made of bone, he was a real piece of work.

When Aunt Celia taught me to crochet, I doubt she knew she was endangering my life.

It's a little known fact that polka dots are the most evil thing in the known universe.

When the sandwich spoke, Steve was not caught completely at unawares.

The Salisbury steak wasn't from Salisbury and it wasn't steak.

Her head hit the floor and bounced once.

The streets of the city were lit by firelight.

It was days like these I regretted having my horns removed.

Derrick aimed a kick right at the thing's grinning face with all the fury of a wet napkin.

He opened his purple umbrella in front of him before it occurred to him that it wouldn't actually protect him from anything.

The rubber ducky may have been yellow, but it was no coward.

Today was the day she got to wear the hat, and wearing the hat was the most important thing in the world.

Blunderbuss is a funny word, but being shot by one steals a lot of the humor from it.

The lava ate through the front door just as I was sitting down to breakfast.

The yellow post-it note I found on my bathroom mirror had a single word written on it.

There was no reason for the creature to respect the screen door, but I was thankful that it did.

I should buy that girl of mine something pretty, I thought bitterly.

She didn't notice the teeth at first because she was too busy trying to decide if it had too many or too few eyes.

Reports of Bigfoot sightings never seem to capture just how rude he is.

My mother always told the end of the story first.

The magnificent swan turned its small head and regarded me judgmentally.

When I fell I had a coffee in each hand, so it was fairly dramatic.

I loved the toile dress that my aunt Mary gave me for my 18th birthday, but nothing attracts bad luck like toile.

The club pulsed with a steady beat that made me feel like I was at the center of a giant heart.

My teacher wouldn't be happy when he got back from his journey and found that I had destroyed the workshop, but I could worry about that later.

The church had named the thing an "abomination," but I was betting it had good qualities too.

I guess Benny didn't believe me when I told him there wasn't enough blood in a human body to fill a ten-gallon aquarium.

Tony stepped forward to make his wish, his one wish.

He snarled as he broke the computer to pieces with the hammer, feeling the joy of doing a job well and completely.

Summoning a demon isn't hard, but it isn't subtle either.

Before the old caretaker left, he told Emily that marshmallows were the answer, but he didn't say to what.

The statue in front of the Columbus City Library hated me

Alex didn't dig trenches because he had to.

The older folks talked about a time when nobody stayed up to keep watch.

What I did was terribly rude, but she ate before the hostess, so you'll understand that I had no choice.

The folks of Chatham County called me "the last hope for red-blooded Americans," but I tried not to get a big head about it.

When I opened my birthday present with a disappointed sigh, I had no idea that the ugly thing would save my life.

The last car to ever pass through the Milner Road tunnel was a sky-blue 1998 Plymouth Acclaim.

This much was clear: the whole security system was fundamentally flawed.

I set my hand against the desk so that the shaking wouldn't spill my coffee.

I couldn't hold on to windowsill anymore, but I couldn't afford to let go.

I'm not sure when humanity thought it would be a good idea to mix its DNA with other creatures, but it was clear fairly quickly that we had been wrong.

Ever since I was six years old I've collected broken clocks.

They weren't scales and they weren't feathers.

The security codes were all in my head, but my head was getting crowded.

My grandfather told me never to open his big, metal thermos.

The brochure tucked under my windshield wiper had nothing on the cover but a big, yellow frowny face.

On the 18th day in a row I woke up with the same song in my head, I started to suspect something was actually wrong, instead of just peculiar.

I looked down at the spatula and thought, here goes nothing.

When I put the deer in my trunk I was positive it was
dead.

She couldn't possibly understand the repercussions of
what she was about to do.

Nobody wants to have to use the word "squirting"
when describing an illness to a medical professional,
but you can't always get what youwant.

The destruction of Earth was probably a tough pill to
swallow for most people.

My dad always said, if you're looking for something
you can't see your best hope is bumping into it.

When I was a kid, the oil and gas smell of the garage meant safety, meant home.

It really bothered me when people called me crazy.

The taco is a cruel mistress.

When the night comes, Brandon will die.

Jack's nightlight went out with a little pop and a puff of smoke.

Vines grew over the door and a tree pushed its branches straight through the roof, the remnants of which lay around the yard like wrapping paper at a kid's birthday party.

Queens was once the center of the paper-fastening universe, home to the greatest stapler and paper clip empires in the world.

The last elephant was in denial.

The animal that jumped from the bushes and into my front bumper was not made of meat.

The crumpled brown paper bag was leaking something.

Everyone makes mistakes, but the blood and vomit on the floor suggested multiple mistakes were made in rapid succession.

From the moment he left the house he'd rehearsed (in his head) walking straight up to them and telling them exactly where they could go (to hell).

Grumplethump had a very silly name and a very serious bite.

Sarah knew that it would be ridiculous for the photos to talk, but whispering seemed like a different matter.

I never thought I would describe a herd of sheep as 'murderous,' but there was a first time for everything.

The tall, angular stranger rounded the corner of my apartment building and handed me a plain, white business card without so much as a word.

I got my bangs cut in a bowling alley bathroom last night.

When the power line broke we kicked the shivering ball of lightning like a white kitten until it mewed and climbed back up the pole and hid in the transformer.

My former commander thought laser-based weaponry was excessive, but he wasn't alive to object anymore.

The devil stretched, curled up in my stomach, and went to sleep.

The ship would have been indistinguishable from a cow, if cows were four stories tall.

I have a clear childhood memory of standing on a wooden dock as the wind snapped the white sails of massive sailing ships and the gulls cried sharp, worried words over the turquoise water, but that is impossible.

My desk drawer didn't contain any office supplies.

The thing that struck me first was the sheer number of tentacles.

It's strange, but I never thought of the cave in the basement wall as unusual.

The human brain now holds the key to our future,
which is why I'm a pessimist.

I could hear, in the distance, the rumble of the walls
coming down.

The columns were all mismatched and the marble was
thirteen different colors, meaning this place had been
repaired dozens of times, quickly and poorly.

Exercising is much easier when something is kind
enough to chase you.

The best kind of traps look like home.

Walking down the hallway that led to the bridge felt like walking down the barrel of a gun.

I wrote the email hours earlier, but I was still eying the send button as if it were a venomous snake.

Let me tell you the exact sound a lead pipe makes when it strikes a grown man's jaw.

A car battery isn't usually considered a toiletry.

Perception without understanding is horror.

Always and *never* lose a lot of their heft when you're not stuck on a single timeline.

One of the greatest accomplishments of my life was getting my pantyhose on this morning, without runs, while wearing glitter nail polish.

Consider the walrus.

"The Monkey's Paw" was an ominous name for a bar, and its location at the end of a dark alley under a single, flickering light didn't exactly inspire confidence, but I'd worked too hard to find it to turn back now.

The tap of her heels on the ground sounded like the ticking of an enormous, cacophonous clock.

The hit men wore black hoodies, black jeans, and clean, white socks.

Flying a starship is a lot like making a meatloaf.

I never did like the man much, but I have to admit that nobody outdrew Gene Black, even drunk off his ass and near dead from pneumonia.

I nearly broke my toe when I kicked the old metal trashcan, but watching it speed down the hill toward the harbor with Luke's body inside really eased the pain.

Plots

Sentient tornadoes seek to seize control of Kansas.

A tiny household robot ineffectually, but fervently, tries to orchestrate a mutiny.

The moon wakes up (and is hungry).

The protagonist has to take a test (genetic, knowledge, truth, etc) that they know they are going to fail.

Our modern notion of personal privacy is a relatively new concept. Envision a future in which insistence on privacy is increased exponentially.

The human race begins to rapidly lose a sense (smell, taste, sight, etc).

Amputated limbs begin regenerating new, whole individuals.

The protagonist finds a stone jug that pours an endless supply of water. He/she tries to monetize it.

Humans have been reduced to doing clerical work for a greater power.

One word: Crocodoodle.

The Earth begins to spin faster. Consequently, everybody weighs less.

Scientists are concerned the acceleration will continue.

Sinkholes appear across the world. People are living on tiny islands of higher land.

A creature is loose in an office building. This creature is tiny, but capable of doing extraordinary damage.

People have developed the ability to fly, but it is a privilege given only to a few.

A monster that eats memories before devouring people physically.

A custom jewelry maker who gains access to his customer's minds when they wear his/her products.

Something that is not water starts raining from the sky.

Neanderthals didn't go extinct. They're transdimensional and some of them are shifting back to our reality.

Computers begin to develop personalities.

All species of insects begin to work together to build a civilization to rival humanity's.

You suddenly have the option to make children mature very rapidly.

Someone dies in a place or time where proper rites cannot be completed.

The President has been mutated and a debate ensues concerning the legitimacy of a non-human presidency.

Scientists accidentally negate friction in a ten-mile radius around a research facility. Rescue team attempts to go in and see what happened.

Your main character investigates a cheating significant other, only to discover a far-reaching conspiracy.

A small door in the back of a closet leads to a mirror image of the protagonist's home and life.

Sitting on a park bench watching a passersby, the protagonist notices one man's shadow is pointing the wrong direction (towards the sun).

Tearing up the carpet while remodeling, homeowners find a message of hope and encouragement referring to a danger that they haven't experienced. Yet.

A nomadic culture on a distant planet, which has never known anything but winter, finds a new route to warmer climates.

People develop a machine that can detect injuries before they happen.

The main character is chosen to be the first ambassador to a newly discovered alien species along with someone else, whom he does not trust. Or like. Not one bit.

Look to the nearest object on your left. That is being used to take over the world.

Every child born after a certain date/time is different from the rest of their species in a significant way. They're still children, so adults can only speculate what the change means long term.

A woman comes to the authorities claiming to be a werewolf and seeking help.

A time traveler arrives in the past (present day) simply to find refuge from a future he hates.

A new breakthrough provides endless power on Earth. The technology is clean and easily reproduced. The necessity to work for basics (food, clean water, power) is mostly negated. The change to the socioeconomic landscape creates new conflicts.

A starlet will rekindle her dwindling fame at any cost, and the cost is turns out to be high.

Transferred to a new school, a student finds that the gym teacher seems to be building a fighting force rather than encouraging general fitness.

A tiny race of insect-like aliens fight a valiant, noble, but ultimately doomed battle against a spaceship's janitorial staff.

A disease appears that seriously affects people's minds, but only temporarily.

Your characters are trapped in a small, secure place (elevator, vault, rowboat).

A bronze age-ish culture holds a certain mountain to be both perilous and sacred. No living person remembers the roots of the tradition. A curious youngster sneaks off to investigate.

Millions of a new kind of creature unexpectedly appear in a single place.

While cleaning out his grandfather's house the protagonist finds a map in a bottle under the floorboards. There is an X marking a spot.

A solar flare/wave of energy/disaster does something catastrophic to exactly half of earth. The unaffected half of the planet has to figure out how to proceed.

A monster that only victimizes people who will not be believed (schizophrenics, dementia sufferers, etc). Its own infeasibility it its greatest defense.

A crew member on a scientific interstellar voyage with no plan for return (or long-term survival) has second thoughts and wants to convince his/her crew members to find a way to turn around.

A modern pharmaceutical company is harvesting ingredients from very (VERY) distant locations. Alien ship? Dimensional portal? Gate to hell? Imagine the list of potential side effects for those drugs.

Vampires capitalize on the current popularity of the undead to prey upon vulnerable fans.

The protagonist purchases or receives a cursed engagement ring.

The protagonist begins to suspect their sibling is involved in a series of violent events.

The protagonist starts working for a mysterious person, whose assistant reminds him a lot of a long-dead friend.

Your protagonist is on a mission of peace to make contact with very sensitive alien race which is easily damaged by certain kinds of human thought.

The technology to create customizable pocket dimensions changes everything on earth. There is nearly limitless land for farming, settlement, etc. What do nations do with the technology? What do individuals do?

Research a historical mystery. Your story should offer an explanation, however improbable.

An archeological discovery hints at an alternative explanation for something.

A supernatural childhood monster (closet/ under the bed) becomes an unlikely ally against a more mundane childhood monster (abusive parent/ bully).

The protagonist very suddenly becomes a leader.

A man wakes on a table in the morgue.

Someone asks the main character to hold something for him. Everyone freaks out about it.

Medical science has found a path to immortality, but it's really only affordable for the super-rich. Consider how this further increases class inequality. What are the long-term implications?

A holiday creature/character is real, and angry.

The protagonist loses his/her wedding ring. He/she has to go somewhere they'd rather not to retrieve it (sewer, haunted house, alien-infested cave).

Humanity invents a time machine and quickly discovers that the best use of it is preventing the invention of the time machine.

A serious of odd dates reveals that a particular online dating service isn't what it seems.

In the future most jobs are done by machines, except two: a human and a dog. The human's job is to feed the dog. The dog is to keep him away from the machines.

The protagonist gets a power that might seem useless at first, like giving their enemies swimmer's ears or wrinkling their pants.

An immortal creature is recruited as a government bureaucrat in orderto give perpetual continuity to a specific job/position.

Humanity makes contact with a "hive mind" type alien race that has difficulty understanding individuality/individual rights and freedoms. This causes various political problems.

The mode of transportation breaks down in the middle of an inhospitable place (space, dessert, mountains, ocean). There are limited resources.

A device that allows plant life to communicate reveals that their thoughts are much more complex than previously believed.

A fortune or prediction comes true, but not in the way the characters thought.

The protagonist finds an unconscious, winged man in a ditch.

A mutated virus makes its host super-human in order to ensure its own survival.

Walking through a forest, the protagonist damages a tree, only to find metal and wires underneath the bark.

The protagonist receives an anonymous package containing an elaborate decoder ring and becomes obsessed with finding a message to decode.

The protagonist runs away from home to live with the mysterious people he sees traveling past his town. The character doesn't need to be a child.

A man decides to build a subterranean kingdom inhabited by (possibly imaginary) inhuman friends and begins digging in his basement.

The protagonist's family has been charged with a sacred duty for thousands of years. Now it's his turn.

An old promise keeps the protagonist from moving out of a disturbingly haunted home.

There is a reason to be afraid of the dark. It's getting worse and humans have changed the way they live to survive.

The protagonist finds a brain in a jar in their attic.

The end of the world is coming, but people have known about it for so long that the initial panic has passed.

The last ruler of a dying planet suggests that if his/her civilization isn't going to survive, it can at least do something memorable.

A game of poker (or other competition) in which every player is psychic, but each believes themself to be the only one with the power.

Technology is so advanced/self-sufficient that humans no longer understand how anything works. Something breaks.

A nutritious, cheap, and easily produced food-product makes starvation a thing of the past, however, prolonged reliance on the product makes regular foodstuffs increasingly difficult to digest. Consider a future in which human reliance on such a product becomes a liability.

A swarm of critters not usually thought of as dangerous or gross (butterflies, bunnies) descends on a town.

Scientists discover an intelligent, isolated, undersea civilization that was unaware of life on land.

Someone famous admits to being an alien.

An electrician called to upgrade an old house finds that the electrical system isn't outdated; it's otherworldly.

Your main character buys a knickknack at a garage sale and quickly begins to suspect that it is stealing from him.

A would-be super hero starts dosing himself with various chemicals/levels of radiation in order to cultivate new powers.

The government requires that all citizens check in multiple times a day via a chip/implant. One day, the protagonist's chip doesn't work.

More and more animals become terrified of the dark and hide under porch lights and street lights. The protagonist tries to find out why.

A woman has chocolates delivered to her apartment, but there's a handgun and a note in the box.

Sorcery has gone corporate. In a world of magic, a manager at an arcane super-store wonders if magic can be anything but boring and industrial.

The protagonist finds what he thinks is an abandoned baby fawn and takes it home, but it's clearly some other kind of creature.

An immortal tries to keep a low profile, but makes herself conspicuous by trying too hard to keep up with current trends.

Challenges

The protagonist's refusal to quit is his/her primary weakness.

The story has a conflicting and never-resolved conception of the central threat/creature.

The protagonist is trying desperately to draw comparisons between his current predicament and his crumbling love life, possibly to find some meaning or solace.

Your narrator is untrustworthy.

Your narrator is trustworthy, but does not trust himself/herself.

Begin with a major climax.

The narrator rejects the lesson trying to be taught to him by the story.

Write your story in letters, texts, tweets, emails, or Facebook posts.

Write a protagonist who is, in all other characters' eyes, the villain.

A character begins to react to events or conversations in a completely unexpected way.

The protagonist has a nervous tick or an obsessive tendency.

Nobody likes to fail. Nobody, but the protagonist.

Create characters that are physically very alien, but easy to relate to.

The protagonist is 87 years old and has arthritis in his knees

Your story is mostly dialogue.

Change a single historical event and set your story in the resulting alternative present.

Write an exciting story in which the hero saves the day through paperwork.

Give an epic feel to a mundane conflict.

You can only use 7 adjectives. Repeats accepted.

No adverbs or adjectives.

Put your characters through scenes with heavy sensory input (loud, cold, bright, etc)

The protagonist doesn't have a complete grasp of the language. They stumble over phrases or create their own odd word groupings. Create your own colloquialisms.

The final climax is totally different from the one the protagonist was preparing for/expecting.

Your protagonist suffers from mental illness, but that fact is not central to the primary conflict.

Your story switches viewpoints at least once.

Write a protagonist that you, yourself, would not like to hang out with.

Write a horror story with no physical violence.

Write a story of 500 words or less with a distinct beginning, middle, and end.

Nobody in your story is clearly good or clearly evil.

An unlikely side character becomes your main protagonist/hero over thecourse of the story.

Write a story from the point of view of the monster/murderer/evil vampire overlord. Humanize them.

The protagonist realizes that something they have done, which they thought was for the best, was actually really hurtful/damaging/wrong. Could be personal or world-changing.

Write a protagonist-against-self story with no other characters.

Read up on a recent scientific finding and make the new discovery crucial to your story.

Human beings can get used to anything. Push that idea to its limits.

Write a short story with a robust magic system (that doesn't bore your reader to tears).

Write a story in which you shed characters and adopt new ones at least twice.

Write a story in first person present tense.

Use short paragraphs and terse sentence structure to create a sense of urgency/breathlessness in your story.

Write a story in which your character is physically very different from the average human. Don't explain or, if you do, keep it as short as possible.

Your story takes place in the span of five minutes or an entire year.

Let the bad guys win.

The protagonist has done something really horrible in the past and everyone knows about it.

Your theme mirrors a real life social issue, but with vampires or aliens or something.

Use a recurring image to reinforce a thematic element of your narrative.

One or more of the characters in your story begin to resemble a stereotype, but then violate the trope in an interesting and unexpected way.

Throw caution, sense, and taste to the wind and write a talking cat story.

Write a repentant, thoughtful antagonist's fall in a way that makes your protagonist seem suddenly distasteful.

Begin your story in one genre and shift to a different genre by the end.

Create a setting that has very specific social rules (where certain people can or can't walk/touch/talk/etc.). Your story should use following/breaking these rules as part of the central conflict.

Your main character is super gross.

Create a very physically/emotional close relationship that is also completely platonic.

Give your story a title that complicates and/or illuminates some aspect of your story.

Create two parallel narratives that converge at the point of climax.

Blur the distinction between what is real and what is not.

Begin your story with an epigraph from a classic (or not so classic) work of fiction or nonfiction. Use it to guide your theme.

Write a secondary world fantasy without using any "info dump" style world-building. In fact, avoid explanation as much as possible.

The story takes place on a mode of transportation (dirigible, car, bike).

Switch points of view throughout your story. (Pay attention to transitions).

Write a story with an omniscient narrator who thinks the whole thing is pretty hilarious.

Your story takes place in several places. Jump between them.

Humanize an inanimate object.

Your character is disabled. The story is not about his disability.

Your story takes place in an unforgiving setting in which management of supplies (water/food) is often the greatest challenge and threat to survival.

Tell your story through a curious observer with limited access to/knowledge of the conflict of the narrative as it unfolds.

Focus on people's clothing, hairstyle, etc. These things can show status, power, or even mental state. Use these to communicate nuances of the plot to the reader.

Pick a genre or style of music. This style provides the theme/feeling for your story.

Your story takes place on a doomed planet racing toward destruction, but the central conflict of the story has little to do with the larger eminent disaster.

Write a conflict in which both sides feel they have won the moral victory by the end of the story.

Your character doesn't particularly like the group/things he's around, but has to deal with it anyway.

The protagonist knows everything about what's going on. The other characters have to drag info out of him.

Your story takes place in seriously extreme weather. You may have to do some research to see how this will affect your characters, vehicles, creatures, etc.

The story begins and ends with the same sentence.

Write a story that fills in the gap between two scenes of a classic novel and/or explores the lives of the minor characters of the novel.

Focus on color in your story. Describe them mostly using senses other than sight.

Pair recognizable names/personalities with alien or fantasy beings/settings.

Your story occurs in at least two historical periods, separated by at least a generation.

The protagonist is 7 months pregnant (with neither an alien nor a demon baby).

Tell the end of the story, then the beginning, then the middle.

Describe in detail the preparing/serving of a meal in a way that sheds light on many aspects of your protagonist's personality.

The protagonist won't state his motivation clearly. Reveal it through his actions.

Write a story that is clearly leading toward a moral, then veers off in a different direction at the last moment.

Write as an historian or a journalist covering the event after it has happened.

Write an allegory.

Go meta. One of the characters knows that he/she is in a story.

In medias res. Start in the middle.

One of your characters only speaks in iambic pentameter.

Write two short sentences as a beginning. Repeat these every 100-200 words. They should have a deeper or different meaning every time they're repeated.

Pepper in punchy two-worders. (They didn't. It wasn't. He fell. Sarah laughed.)

Find a poem or song you like. Weave the lyrics into your story.

Write a story with characters who are geographically linked and weave their stories together. For example, every house on a cul-de-sac.

Borrow a fairy tale trope and skew it in a novel way to add another layer of meaning to the narrative.

Take an old saying and invent an origin for it.

Your character loses, or has recently lost a sense (sight, hearing, even touch). The struggle to cope with the loss complicates your central conflict.

Write from the perspective of a child. They may not understand everything they see.

Write a story with two endings that contradict each other.

The protagonist is bilingual and occasionally switches languages (without alienating readers).

Write the same scene from three different angles. Reveal and complicate the truth about what is actually happening with each new telling.

Write a humorous story in first person in which your protagonist has no intent to be funny.

ABOUT THE AUTHORS

Leslie and Jarod Anderson's work has appeared in world-class speculative markets including *Asimov's, Strange Horizons, Andromeda Spaceways Inflight Magazine, Escape Pod*, and *Daily Science Fiction*. Leslie has an MA in poetry and an obsession with ponies and rocket ships. Jarod has an MA in literature and a tattoo of John Milton on his right bicep.

www.jarodkanderson.com
www.lesliejanderson.com

4245848R00043

Printed in Great Britain
by Amazon.co.uk, Ltd.,
Marston Gate.